Chocolate Mixer

Jason Armstrong

This book is for two little people who help me see the magic and wonder in even the simplest things...my children.

To the Reader

While making her favorite snack with her Daddy, little Sofia makes an amazing discovery about herself!
Her realization changes the way she sees this colorful world. Filled with wonder and questions,
Sofia journeys into a world that isn't just black or white, but a beautiful rainbow of colors.

This book is the story of a little girl learning that she is Multiracial.

'Chocolate Mixer' addresses the common questions our children may ask about a world filled with
different cultures, skin-colors and ways of life, and how even our own parents can look so different
from one another.

Published by Waldorf Publishing
2140 Hall Johnson Road
#102-345
Grapevine, Texas 76051
www.WaldorfPublishing.com

Chocolate Mixer
ISBN: 9781942846482
Library of Congress Control Number: 2015934201
Copyright © 2015

I have a little brother
He's chocolate
mixer too

We love to play together
In mommy's and daddy's shoes

My best friend is vanillia
We like to play all day

I love him oh so much
I'm happy when
he spends the night

Every day I find new things
That are chocolate mixer like me

He sat me at the table
And got my little cup

I wondered to myself
What is he going to do

My milk turned chocolate mixer
Right before my eyes

My very favorite treat
In the whole wide world

Is chocolate mixer too
Like mommy's and daddy's
favorite boy and girl

My mommy says lots of things are mixer
To see them I just have to look around

My daddy says everyone is some kind of mixer
From grandma and nonna on down

He sat me on his lap
and said "my rainbow you see"
We are all some kind of mixer,
just look at a family

Every child is one part mommy
And one part daddy too

So you always get the best of both
How lucky are me and you

I really
like being
chocolate
mixer
This is
very
true

Most of all
I love me
for me
And you
for just
being
you.

Jason Armstrong was born and raised in Brooklyn, New York. While going to school to pursue a degree in physical therapy he was recruited and hired by a communications company as a specialist. He quickly rose through the ranks to become an acting team leader and corporate reinvention leader. While still employed in the corporate world, his interest in health & wellness lead him to pursue a career in personal training.

Being an entrepreneur at heart and not wanting to stop there, he went on to join the U.S. Air Force reserve to be trained in nutritional medicine while still attending school to get a degree in occupational sciences. This enabled him to work as a massage therapist and shortly after that he began teaching massage at a school in Manhattan.

Jason then decided to pursue his dream of opening his own wellness center, which led to him moving to Italy. It was here that he started to develop his love for photography, the saxophone and wine. While living in Italy with his two children, his love for writing, which had been dormant for sometime, resurfaced when his daughter innocently had an epiphany over some chocolate milk.

Up until this time his writing had mainly consisted of poetry, of which a few poems were published in local corporate newspapers. After successfully opening up a wellness center in the Tuscan region of Italy, his love of wine met with an opportunity to launch his own startup importing wines and spirits into America, which lead him to moving back to New York.

While focusing on his start-up and returning to teaching, the thought of publishing this one particular book still sat in his head. Although by no means a professional author, he felt the message was important, but mostly he wanted to do it as a tribute and out of love for his two children.

Jason Armstrong currently lives in Brooklyn, New York and spends his time pursuing his passion for teaching, running his wine importing business and publishing his first children's book.